**ONCE YOU GET FAR
ENOUGH AWAY,
YOU'RE ON YOUR
WAY BACK HOME**

ONCE YOU GET FAR ENOUGH AWAY, YOU'RE ON YOUR WAY BACK HOME

ANTHONY HUERTA VELASQUEZ

Mouthfeel Press is a bilingual indie press. We publish poetry, fiction, and non-fiction. Our print books are available through independent bookstores and online booksellers, or at author's readings.

CLASH! Chapbook Series is an imprint of Mouthfeel Press.

Cover Art and Design by Cloud Cardona
Interior Design: Kimberly James

Contact Information:
info.mouthfeelbooks@gmail.com

ISBN: 978-1-957840-39-0

Published in the United States, 2024
First Printing in English
$12

For Susanna MacLaren and Nellie Velasquez, every day

Contents

World Cup Identity

A Chicano living in South Korea sometimes feels like a time-traveling California Yanqui in King Sejong's Court. At least during my first year teaching there, if you're brown, you were probably asked the same questions and were in many similar conversations with Korean natives that went something like this:

"Ah, nice to meet you. Where you from?"

"California."

"Ooohhhh! But you have dark hair, dark eye?"

"Yeah, well there's many different kinds of people there from all over the world. Have you ever been to LA? There are many people there that look like you. And they're Americans, Californians too."

"Ah, LA! You like Koreatown?"

"I'm not from LA, but Koreatown is very cool."

"You like baseball? You know Park Chan-ho?"

"Yeah, Chan-ho was a great pitcher." (We ignore Chan-ho's humiliating highlights as a Dodger: giving up historic home runs to Barry Bonds. Kicking opposing pitcher Tim Belcher of the Angels. Serving up two grand slams to Fernando Tatis *in the same inning!* Show respect. Save Face.)

"You can eat spicy food? You like kimchi?"

"Yes. I like it very much."

"Good! How old are you?"

"Thirtysomething."

"You married?"

"Nah."

"Why no marry?"

"Well, that's a long story I guess."

"Ah, ok! Playboy, one shot!"

"Ha! Thanks. *Geonbae!*"

Yet, every four years, a new question would often come up. This time not from the locals but from some friendly *waygukin* or foreigners.

"Hey Anthony, hope you don't mind me asking, I know you're American but still, just wondering: Who do you root for in the World Cup? What if USA is playing Mexico?"

"No, I don't mind."

* * *

There's a kind of dust and desolation you only find along California State Route 43, the old Central Valley Highway. Driving down the 99 just past Fresno, veer right at Selma, "The Raisin Capital of the World." Over one hundred years of Sun Maid raisins and myriads of sun mad toils in the vineyards is where the 43 begins. Another thirty-five miles south between the cotton, alfalfa, corn fields, and dairies, you'll find where I'm from: Corcoran, California.

My first home was Corcoran. A town at the heart of the apple strikes fictionalized in John Steinbeck's *In Dubious Battle* in the 1930s, but made real and factionalized by the cotton strikes of my grandfathers in the '60s. A place where Cesar Chavez is both celebrated and reviled. My grandpa Lawrence lionized the United Farm Workers efforts. To my grandpa Jimmy, however, Chavez was a *mojado*, a wetback, an agitator whitewashed by the communists when he just wanted a job and a paycheck to bring home for my grandma and my mother.

Though it's a good two and a half hour drive to the Central Coast, the dust there is like sand from the beach lodged under the nail of your big toe: you can do all you can to rinse it off, try to fully rid yourself of it, but it's always there. It'll suddenly and subtly appear in the strangest of faraway places.

* * *

After my family left Corcoran for, by San Joaquin Valley standards, the posh big city of Visalia, population of fifty thousand , gateway to Sequoia National Park, it was a reversal of where I was born; except on the northside redolent with taquerías and panaderías, practically everyone was white. Where one question, especially in elementary school, annoyed me until my end of days there:

"What are you? "

"I'm American."

"No, I mean, what are you? What kind of American are you?"

"I'm American. Ok, I'm Californian."

"No, I mean, where is your family from?"

"My parents were born in California. My grandparents were born here, too."

"No, I mean, are you Spanish, Mexican, Chinese? I don't know, what are you?"

"Well, my parents and grandparents speak both Spanish and English but I can't speak Spanish. My great-grandparents, grandparents, and, at times, even my parents have all had to pick cotton at some point. But I'm not doing that. I had my baptism and first communion at St. Mary's but I'm no longer going to catechism. Sure, we eat enchiladas and tamales for Christmas but you're never going to find a better turkey and stuffing for Thanksgiving than my mom's."

"Haha, I heard that about your mom. I heard that she's good for stuffing."

"Fuck you, Matt."

"Haha, come on Tony, it's a joke. Speaking of jokes, I got one. Why do Mexicans eat tamales for Christmas?"

"I don't know."

"So you have something to unwrap."

Fuck off, Scott. And my name's not Tony.

Come middle school, high school, there was a different kind of awareness and identity that I was confronted with on a daily basis. Outside the boys bathroom was an intimidating wall of bussed-in vatos and cholos that made me evade their gambit and their epithets, such as pocho, maricon, or joto, just for me to take a leak. In college, girls from La Raza would call me a 'coconut' (brown on the outside, white on the inside) or a 'Mexican't' (can't speak Spanish and certainly cannot dance).

* * *

With the U.S. hosting the 1994 World Cup, my identity and rooting interest were definitely questioned. Do I root for my home country's team that fielded players with presidential looks like Captain John Harkes and the footballing hippie-looking ginger Alexi Lalas? Or do I root for Jorge Campos, the high-flying Mighty Mouse of a goalkeeper, and the cagey veteran Marcelino Bernal, especially with Bernal being a family name? Tired of the insults that made me feel like an inferior American because of my skin, I wanted to see some brown people victorious over the honkies so I donned the jersey of El Tri. Though Mexico was historically the odds-on favorite in regards to soccer, we still felt like an underappreciated underdog versus America in anything, especially on their home turf. Therefore, ¡Viva México!

This continued on through the Campos and 'El Matador' Luis Hernandez years. Until one day, I found myself at an English pub on Koh Samui, Thailand, where I caught the 2009 Confederations Cup U.S. versus Spain semifinal, a switch was flipped.

A Thai local saw me watching the game with great interest. He approached me and asked, "Where are you from?"

"Uh, I guess I'm Mexican but I'm from California?"

"Ok. But where are you from? Are you from Mexico?"

"No. I'm from the States."

"Is your passport from Mexico?"

"No, I have an American passport."

"Well then, that's it. You are American."

* * *

Growing up back then when all that mattered was Pop Warner football and Future Farmers of America, Hard Rock Cafe t-shirts, Wranglers, or Guess Jeans, where it was all about jocks, preps, and shit-kickers; it was hard to fit in to that kind of all-American youth. Or feel Mexican really, for that matter. It wasn't until I got to Asia that I truly felt American. *What's your passport?* USA. No more questions asked. Further, actually, it answers the follow-up: Why Korea?

For this emigrant whose ancestors originated south of the border but chose to settle west of the Sun, it's that I simply no longer have to answer the question, *What are you?* I'm American. Also, perhaps I just wanted to go someplace where status is not determined by how big your ranch is, your ski cabin in the Sierras, or your speedboat. That it really doesn't matter how many acres, horses, pickups, or Mexicans your family owns. And I could never subscribe to this "Love it or leave it" notion, the predominant either/or mentality. You can love it *and* leave it.

There's also the fact that I'm allergic to dust.

Right between Waukena, population 108, and Corcoran, is the cemetery. My great-grandparents from my maternal side are buried there, my grandparents from both sides rest there, and scores more of my Mexi-kin. Yet, I'm allergic to that dust. But one day, I probably will return there. Should return there. I hope to return to that dust. But, God willing, not today.

As-Salaam Alaikum, Moustafa

October 24, 2010. Tramping down Ramses Street, I felt strangely at home. The sidewalks were filled with vendors selling car parts, imitation designer clothing, knockoffs of popular toys, used books, old magazines, and mounds of cassettes. Strolling along, perusing the wares, it reminded me of being a boy at the flea market with my grandfather. Or the *remate* as he called it in his Mexican-Spanish. I raked through piles of tapes but didn't find any James Brown, The Commodores, Rick James, Vicente Fernandez, or Los Tigres del Norte. The music of my childhood was absent, but that process of digging took me back.

I wandered for hours on wide avenues around well-groomed traffic circles and through narrow, pot-holed, shadowy alleys beneath the domes and minarets awash in the colors of the desert itself. The architecture in the central district was a pastiche of Belle Époque, Renaissance Revival, '60s Mod, and urban decay painted from the same palette of sand, smoke, and grime. *This is the Paris of the Nile?* I thought. I turned down an oil-slicked strip of hardware stores and mechanic shops and found a food cart offering pitas filled with crispy falafels, grilled eggplant, lentils, baba ghanouj, and fresh chopped parsley for one Egyptian pound. About twenty-five cents.

I ate three of them and stashed a couple for later. I soon began to get accustomed to the incessant honking of impetuous vehicles and the blaring of lo-fi recordings of the *adhan* from the loudspeakers of mosques. I heard the call to prayer as an invocation so I ventured further on past sidewalk cafes, tempted by the sweet, heavily scented puffs of the hookah, which mixed with car emissions, makes for quite a heady waft. I think I'm going to like this place, I thought. *Inshallah.* God willing.

* * *

Dusk fell rapidly on the Qasr El Nil Bridge as the sun set behind the west bank of the Nile illuminating a pink and orange-brown sky over Tahrir Square. The promenade outside the Museum of Egyptian Antiquities replete with palm trees under such smog reminded me of LA, but the sphinxes and Old Kingdom sculptures of pharaohs were otherworldly. I pressed on but soon found what I'm always looking for in any destination: a friendly watering hole. Off the main circle between Talaat Harb Street and El Tahrir, a long, narrow, wooden building stood alone. It was calling me with its circular yellow sign featuring a blue star and blue script in English advertising "Stella" above its red door and green frame.

I pushed through a pair of swinging saloon doors, and sensing that it was a real locals only type of place, it felt like the record just scratched, the music stopped, and all eyes were on me. But just for a moment. I soon realized that the three dozen Cairenes, all men, occupying the dark wooden tables in this veritable dive seemed to embody the same mentality as the cops on the beat in Juarez, Mexico. As in Bob Dylan's "Just Like Tom Thumb's Blues": it's best you don't need them because they certainly don't need you there.

I sidled up to a stool at the bar through the billowing cigarette smoke, admiring the craftsmanship of the mahogany and glass cabinetry, and set my luggage down on the hardwood floor. The bartender was a heavy-set old man with silver whiskers on his face and even less hair atop his head. Maybe it was the way his skin shone like polished bronze with a round, protruding belly like a Buddha, or the way his wide nostrils flared at the end of a preternatural proboscis, or maybe it was the way everyone glanced up from their drinks, scanned the stranger, and went right back to their business; I felt like I had just entered the Mos Eisley cantina on Tatooine.

The bartender trudged over. He studied me up and down with a folded brow and pursed lips. I offered him a cheery "Hello." He responded with a stern, deep "Hal-lo." When I ordered a bottle of beer he seemed to labor to get it out of the clear glass fridge and served it begrudgingly. He said something I didn't understand to which I stammered, "I'm sorry, I. . . " so he flashed nine digits. I handed over the exact amount and he snatched it with his right hand then began rubbing the tips of a thumb to the index and middle fingers of his left hand. "Teeps," he muttered. I handed over three more pounds and the man lit up in a Nile-wide smile. He slapped the bar and quickly presented me two small tin plates. One of hominy, one of arugula leaves, fished up from under the counter. Then he grabbed my wrist as if he was shaking my hand and bounced over to his barstool.

I sat there grazing on the happy hour snacks, washing them down with the room-temp Egyptian lager, until I heard someone calling for attention coming from one of the tables. "Hey! Hey buddy! Hey friend!" I glanced to the left, to the right, then heard another, "Hey friend!" coming from right behind me. I swiveled around and saw a man with a pale complexion who looked to be about my age. Thirty-five. Maybe a couple years younger. "Hey, come here. Have drink with me. Please." I gathered my things and sat down at his table by the front door.

"Yes, sit down. This place is good not bad," he said with Arabic-accented English. "Do you smoke?" He displayed a hardpack of Marlboro Reds in his hand. I leaned over the armrest so I could retrieve my pack from a front pocket and waved it to him.

"Yes," he nodded, then belted out a slightly altered Mick Jagger lyric, "Because he can't be a man if he cannot smoke the same cigarettes as me! I can't get no—"

"Satisfaction," I said.

"Yes. Satisfaction. Marlboro is good not bad." He lit one up, took a drag, and said, "I am Moustafa."

I shook his hand, "I'm Anthony."

"Antony, yes. Like Mark Antony." I didn't bother to correct his pronunciation of my name. "Let me see, you . . . American?"

"Yeah, I'm from California."

"California. Yes. It's good not bad." He seems like a nice person and he knows The Stones but how many times is he going to say something is good not bad, I wondered as I lit up a Red of my own. "You know, you look like you can be Egyptian," he said.

"Really?"

"Oh, yes. You have brown skin and dark beard, you look like you can be Egyptian, maybe Syrian. Jordan. That's goo— "

"Thanks!" I interjected. I hoisted my glass of Stella. Moustafa raised his glass of domestic brandy and mineral water. "Cheers!"

Moustafa told me he was a native of Cairo and a public school history teacher. He fit the bill with his short sleeve, button up plaid shirt tucked into his khakis. He had an easygoing demeanor and was curious to know more about my first year teaching in Korea. We sat there for quite a while talking about our jobs, favorite soccer teams, music, and our hometowns. We both shared a real fondness for the Mexican National World Cup teams of the '90s, led by their Mighty Mouse of a goalkeeper Jorge Campos and their lone striker Luis 'El Matador' Hernández. Then he sang me some tunes by his favorite artists, like The Bee Gees, Roxette, Phil Collins, George

Michael, and Elton John. I added a timely, "Bay-bey!" to his short rendition of George Michael's "Faith," softly accompanied him with the chorus of "Careless Whisper," and we alternated lines to a few Sir Elton songs. After the tiny bar table acapella concert, the conversation drifted back to native grounds. I had to dispel the myth for him that California is all Baywatch and Disneyland. He told me of places I must visit around Cairo outside of the downtown core and the pyramids. Every now and then we paused and took turns buying rounds. Perhaps the spirits allowed him to relax the rules of social norms. I had read that talk of politics should be avoided in Egypt, especially in public, so I was surprised when Moustafa broached a sensitive subject.

"You know, I think we are the same. You love your home and I love my home. But, you are American. You are lucky. I live here and our government is very bad. Mubarak is very bad."

"I'm sorry, I know Mubarak is president but I don't know all that much about him."

"He does not care for anyone but his own ass and the people who kiss his ass. He does not care about the people, the working people, he only cares about the people who work for him. He does not care about people. He only cares about money. And he only helps the people with money." (Recalling what Moustafa said about Mubarak's Egypt over a decade ago now sounds prophetic: that's America under the 45th President and the GOP today.) As soon as he extinguished the butt in the ashtray, he lit up another. I was moved by his honest opinions and I could sense his frustration, but I thought perhaps, for both of us, it's best we talk about something else. But before I could lighten the mood, he reiterated, "You are so lucky you live in America."

I guess the beer and brandy loosened my tongue as well. "You know, Moustafa, things aren't as great as they seem. You know we had eight years of George Bush and—"

"Yes, fuck Bush. But, you are so rich. You live in Korea. You go to Thailand. You go to Europe. You have American passport. You can go anywhere." I tried to explain to him that, yes, I am lucky, but so many in my country aren't so fortunate. Also, I wanted him to understand that, yes, the American passport is powerful but all the rights and privileges aren't distributed equally. I thought he would be a sympathetic ear for the problems I had before I arrived here in Cairo because of certain phenotypes I possess. Two weeks prior, I was the target of a so-called "random passport check" in Koblenz, Germany at the train station where my passport was confiscated and I was sequestered by three police officers. That delay, for no reason other than traveling while brown, caused me to miss my connection. Travel beard backfire number one. Then at the Athens airport earlier that morning, an act of kindness backfired. I assisted an old Palestinian man struggling with his luggage. He had difficulty pulling his suitcase along the tiled floor while dragging his gimpy left foot with the aid of his wooden cane. I was interrogated by security officers before boarding for helping that man. I was accused of aiding and abetting an illegal, or possibly a terrorist. How could I have known that he was blacklisted from flying? My Americanness only goes so far. I tried to tell him, when you look like someone from south of the border, Northern Africa, the Middle East, or really anyone not white, there is a caveat that comes with that US passport. Not to mention the racial profiling and the indignities some citizens must endure back in the States for simply DWBB: Driving While Black or Brown. But Moustafa stopped me there.

"Were you arrested?"

"No," I answered.

He finished his glass of brandy in one gulp, took a deep drag, sucking into a wide grimace. "You see, you have American passport. You have Get Out Of Jail Free card. And do you think I can go to your country? I work, I am a teacher but do you think I can make the money to go to your country? If I had the money, you think they will let me in? I have looked. All the shit, the hoops I have to do to get the visa to see your country. It's shit!" He snuffed out his cigarette and poured another drink. He stared down at his glass shaking his head from side to side, before looking me right in the eye and said, "I like you. I like you, Antony, but . . . fuck your first world problems."

* * *

I hadn't noticed that the bartender was watching us intently during our conversation. I guess he could feel the tension in the room. He said something to Moustafa from across the bar. Moustafa waved a hand in the air a couple of times. I can only surmise from his gestures that everything's alright. Inshallah. Moustafa then shook his head in the affirmative and eased a grin at me. "You know, he is a good man. That man there, he can only say two words in English. 'Hello' and 'tips,' but he is a good man. And if you tip him well, he will do anything for you. He will open his ass for you."

"Well, I'm a good tipper but I don't think I need that."

"Well, you might not need it, but he does."

I put my elbow on the table and rested my forehead in my palm. I tried to focus on the wall and swallow an outburst of laughter that was about to explode. Moustafa laughed while reaching across the table to grab my arm. He patted the top of my free hand and clutched his highball glass. I grabbed mine and we gently clinked them.

"Fe sahetek," he said.

"Salud," I replied.

* * *

"What about movies, Antony, you like movies?" he asked.

"Well, I'm not a big movie guy, but sure, I like movies."

"You see *Lucky Number Slevin*? You see *12 Monkeys*?"

"No, I've heard of them but I haven't seen them."

"What about *Die Hard*?"

"Oh, yeah. I've seen that. That one's great."

"Yes! Yippee-ki-yay, motherfucker. I love Bruce Willis. Ok! Bruce Willis is good not bad. But, you see the movie *Thelma & Louise*?"

"Funny you should ask," I said. "My uncle used to be, tried to be an actor. His biggest role, the only time he made it on screen, was in *Thelma & Louise*. He was one of the cops in the end. He was on screen for just a second. He's the cop, the bald guy, sitting down, who hands the phone to the lead detective. To Harvey Keitel."

Moustafa's eyes grew wide then welled up with joy and astonishment. He set down his glass, clenched a fist, shook it vigorously before pounding the table, exclaiming, "I know this man!" His hands trembled as he reached in his box for another cigarette. I saw a tear streak down his cheek as he lit it. "I know this man! I have seen this movie one thousand times. Oh, I cannot believe I am sitting here with you, drinking with this man from *Thelma & Louise*!"

"I was not in *Thelma & Louise*, my uncle was," I reminded him.

"No. No. That does not matter. You are family with man from my favorite movie, *Thelma & Louise*. Bring him to Egypt, please! I must meet your uncle. I must meet this man. You close to him?"

"Yeah, he's the best."

"Ok, Antony, let's go," he said. "I want to take you somewhere.

Let's get Turkish coffee and sheesha. I treat you. *Yalla!*" After our night cap, Moustafa led me to a place not far from the bar up on Talaat Harb Street. It was a family-owned guest house of a flat on the second floor in a veritable rundown, Victorian flophouse. It was perfect. He roused the owner, helped me check in, and then took off.

My plan was to stay in Cairo for three days but ended up staying there for nine. During the day, I toured Old Town Coptic Cairo and the Saladin Citadel. One day, I took a tour of Saqqara and out to Giza where I rode a horse with no name around the pyramids. Other days I walked through Tahrir Square, strolled along the Corniche Nile, and visited the Egyptian Museum. Except for the one night, though, when I dined on a mixed-grill of quail, lamb chops, and kofta, with an eggplant and chickpea salad, French fries, and a bottle of Lebanese red wine at the legendary Café Riche, I met Moustafa at our bar every night. But when he invited me to his family's house up in the country to the north, I knew it was time for me to depart. Other than happy hours and bar time, I'm not very good with plans and commitments. I'm especially not very good with goodbyes. I shipped out on an overnight bus to the Sinai Peninsula. I got off in Dahab, a little hippie town east of Mount Moses and the Burning Bush over on the Red Sea coast. *Shokran*, Cairo. Thank you.

* * *

January 25, 2011. I was shocked by the evening news on TV of fifty thousand protesters against President Hosni Mubarak descending on Tahrir Square three months to the day since my arrival in Cairo. Over the next eighteen days, I was obsessed with the reports from the BBC, Al Jazeera, and the videos I saw on CNN and PBS. First there were the videos of men on horses and camels cracking whips parting through the masses assembled there. Then the footage of unarmed civilians being beaten, being runover by personnel carriers, citizens dying at the hands of the state. Next were the armored vehicles and tanks rolling into the site while military helicopters and warplanes flew overhead during the day. That was followed by the firing of tear gas and lethal bullets from riot police as activists threw molotov cocktails and rocks at them throughout the night. The neighborhood mosque I passed daily was doubling as a makeshift hospital for the wounded. Tragic scenes unfolding right on the very streets I had just traversed, in front of the very places I had visited as the number of participants downtown swelled up into the hundreds of thousands. It was all too surreal for me to believe what was transpiring. But in reality, considering what Moustafa said about Mubarak and the Egyptian government, should I or the world really be all that shocked?

Every video or photo I saw, I examined with grave concern looking for Moustafa's face in the crowd. I wanted to reach him, write him a letter (still do) but I lost the bar napkin which he wrote his address on. I'm terrible at organizing info and keeping contacts, and even worse at keeping in touch. I left Cairo for Dahab, Jerusalem, and Amman, then was off to Kuala Lumpur, Bali, and Bangkok, eventually returning to California. Back to the San Joaquin Valley, to my parents' middle class, three-bed/two-bath ranch house, watching a revolution that *was* televised, heartbroken by growing fear for my friend's safety, and helplessly feeling like a rich, privileged spoiled American, somewhat guilty, utterly rudderless in life.

* * *

Moustafa, if you ever get to read this, I want you to know I'm sorry. I still owe you a signed headshot of my uncle from his acting days. Believe me, I have not forgotten. I really hope you are well, buddy, and wish you all the best. *Ila al-liqaa, as-salaam alaikum.* Until we meet again, peace be unto you. *Inshallah.* God willing.

Frequently Asked Questions about Staying Safe in
South Korea

1. What was that?

I awoke from a sonic boom thunderclap to see fresh contrails so close they streaked the bedroom window of my high-rise apartment. A fighter jet? I don't know. Whatever it was left only long white traces in the blue sky between the coastal range and the sea. I saw that the traffic on Gwangan Bridge over Suyeong Bay was at a standstill while buses, sedans, taxis, and scooters raced amid incessant horn blasts on the thoroughfare below. Morning commute, business as usual. But on that day, something really unnerved me.

When I first moved to South Korea, fall 2009, there was something comforting about seeing US naval ships dock here, back when everything felt so foreign. Walking around the city I'd see young couples with identically matched t-shirts, shorts, socks, and sneakers; young ladies strutting in high-heels with a cell phone outstretched in one hand, turning the handicap accessible paths over the sand at Haeundae Beach into a fashion show catwalk; men of all ages clad in hospital-issued pajamas, smoking while pushing mobile IV stands on their way to buy cheap coffee from take-out windows; poodles, pomeranians, and bichons with ears dyed hot pink or lime green wearing sequined sweatshirts and colorful doggy booties; and octopuses with dreams of cephalopod emancipation climbing out of small kiddie pools for a very brief stroll on the wet pavement in the alleys of the Jagalchi Fish Market. All of this used to seem so strange. So when sailors were teeming these shores on leave from vessels flagged with the Stars and Stripes, they represented something recognizable, familiar, conspicuous reminders of home.

Nowadays though, life in Busan, which was once strange, has become mundane. However, as Pyongyang prepares to ignite "an unimaginable sea of fire" and launches test missiles that soar over Hokkaido, the White House considers a "bloody nose" strike and boasts of "bigger buttons." In the time of brinkmanship, spotting the USS Nimitz or the USS Ronald Reagan out my window no longer provides the same comfort and security I once felt when I first saw them in the harbor.

2. Is it safe there?

Before I lived in Busan proper, I landed in the outskirts across the Nakdong River in a quiet, brand new condo subdivision. Before I learned about Skype and realized I could pop into a *PC bang* to video chat with loved ones for a thousand *won* per hour (about a dollar), I'd drop a *man cheon won*, a green ten-thousand note, on a calling card from the Family Mart. At the counter, I'd show the clerk my phone. Then I would gesture with my forefinger and thumb on the other hand as if I were a bouncer inspecting a driver's license. "Card-uh for *miguk* call," I'd say, stammering in Konglish, hoping he'd understand. *Miguk* and *maekju*, America and beer, being the only *Hangeul* words I knew back then. The young man would then retrieve a long narrow shoe box from under the counter containing stacks of various calling cards featuring different colors and flags. Each time I bought one was like buying lotto scratchers at a gas station. Some offered up to 110 minutes of calls from the Republic of Korea to the US. Some only 37 minutes. Once or twice, none at all. When I did get through to my mom, conversations always started with, "Hi mijo! How are you? I'm glad you called. I just read something in the news. You really think it's safe there?"

3. *What's it like over there?*

My friends back home word it a little differently than my parents but are really asking the same thing: *What's it like over there in Korea with, you know, Kim Jong-il?* Later, *Kim Jong-un?* Or simply, *the North?* A question I've been asked countless times over the years that I've never been able to consistently answer. Usually, though, I'd remind my friends and family that the peninsula is not just divided but still technically at war, yet people don't live in fear. They just go about their daily lives. And if you ask the locals, most will tell you that whatever belligerent rhetoric from the North that is reported by the American media ends up being a much bigger deal to Americans than it does to them. They ignore the Supreme Leader's bellicose rants since they've been hearing such provocations for over sixty years. So it goes.

4. Are you sure it's safe there?

For being Korea's second-city, a metropolis of four million, it's quite a walkable city. Though it's not as compact as San Francisco, Busan is packed with its peaks, beaches, and bridges that remind me of The City. But when people ask, *Are you safe there?* I tell them my only fear is being run over. Run over by the motorcycle riders and delivery men on scooters who believe the sidewalk is a diamond lane. A friend of mine suffered a broken leg and some cracked ribs from being hit by a KyoChon Chicken driver on a speeding moped. For that reason, my wife Susanna no longer uses her iPod when walking to and from work. I, on the other hand, put music on low and recall what my lacrosse coach said about playing defense, "Check man. Check ball. Head on a swivel!"

More dangerous, though, are the Audi, BMW, Mercedes, and taxi drivers. As to the former, those with the German imports, with money comes impunity. I wait three full seconds before stepping off a curb, watching them blur by under a red light. I pause even longer when a taxi is approaching. Even then, just when I've almost completely made it across, a scooter may be passing a bus on the right, hidden from sight, trying to get a jump on the traffic, blowing through the red. Hence, check ahead, check behind, both sides, constantly. Head on a swivel.

One day I was walking down by Gwangalli Beach. Crossing the street, over half way through the crosswalk with the green man giving me the right of way, I noticed the driver of a black Jaguar had decided to proceed making his right turn while looking down at the phone in his palm. An older lady was holding hands with her twenty-something daughter under a parasol. They took two steps then jumped back to safety on the curb. I stopped in the middle of the intersection, pissed that the man driving still did not look up to notice me a mere foot away, so I slapped the driver-side back window with my left hand. The smack of my tungsten wedding ring made the sound of glass cracking. The daughter, now saucer-eyed, made a ring with her mouth, then gasped with an audible "Oh!" The jagoff passed the corner restaurant with its tanks of live eel, squid, and flatfish, then he stopped in the middle of the road. My inclination was to run but thought that would definitely exhibit guilt, so I quickly put my head down and picked up my pace in long strides weaving between tourists and beachgoers until I ran up the stairs to an expat bar on the fourth floor.

Ten minutes later, K showed up. When I told him about my near miss, my kind of hit and run, he repeated what my girlfriend-now-wife has been telling me for years, "You are a *waygukin*. A foreigner. Remember there are two types of judicial systems here: one for natives and one for foreigners. And if the two are mixed up in a dispute, ninety percent of the time, the native wins. So, yeah, keep your head on a swivel, but keep your hands to yourself. Got it?"

"Fine," I said. "You're right." We knocked back our pints and settled into another round. "Alright, you've been here a long time, so let me ask you something then — how do you respond when people ask you 'How's it going over there? You staying safe over there?'"

"Yeah, people always ask that, right? I get messages all the time on Facebook from my family, friends in Indiana, saying, 'That crazy fat man over there's building nuclear bombs. We pray for you. Stay safe over there, Kenneth May.' To which, I try not to get into it, but sometimes I message back, 'I read six people were murdered over Memorial Day weekend in Indianapolis. To put it in perspective, six people shot, killed in Indianapolis over the holiday. That's more than all the murders in Busan last year.' So, I just got to say to them, 'Stay safe over there, too!'"

5. *When are you coming home?*

Recently, at the height of all the sabre-rattling from both sides, I woke up to see a simple message pop up in my gmail. It was from my older brother who lives in Bakersfield. He wrote, "Stop the madness and come home! Get home safe!"

He's telling me to come home, I thought. I read that in Bakersfield last night two victims died of gunshot wounds at Kern Medical Center. Local NBC-affiliate KGET news is reporting, "Halfway through 2018, homicides in Kern County outpacing 2017 killings." Yet he's telling me to "Stop the madness!" Considering the scourge of gun violence across the States these days, I wanted to tell him don't worry about me or tell me to come home — *you should worry about your own damn safety!* But I didn't.

Instead, I replied, "You know, California will always be home to me, just like New York is home to Susanna, but Busan is *our* home. Why don't you come visit sometime and see for yourself? This place isn't so strange, so crazy. It's home. Hope you're good, Brother. Stay safe, too.

Annyeong to All That

"It is easy to see the beginning of things,
and harder to see the ends."

- Joan Didion

Even today, I can remember the visceral unease of anticipation and the disquieting loneliness that set in when my life abroad began. While reading the instructions on how to prepare the *bibimbap* served on my flight, I remember how easy it was to remain afloat with that head-in-the-clouds excitement, embarking on what I thought would be a novel year-long sojourn for reasons I clearly didn't know back then. All I knew was this: I was thirty-four years old, had quit a dozen jobs, finally graduated after sixteen years of college just to obtain a bachelor's degree, and hoped that if I could find my bearings in the Orient, perhaps I'd be able to find a sense of direction in my life. But from the glimmer of a dawn on the horizon west of the sun, ideas and plans that were initially formed out of mere abstraction started to make sense. That is, moving to Korea made sense until I landed on the ground.

On the stretch of road from the airport past the duck farms along the south bank of the Nakdong River to my assigned housing in

New Myeongji Ocean City Queendom English Town, what first struck me was that the only English I saw was on the gas stations, the no-tell motel moral holiday inns, and the billboards effervescing *Korea Sparkling!*; everything else was expressed in glowing neon Hangeul and I was illiterate. When out encountering locals speaking in their native tongue, I reverted to Spanish by default which didn't help anyone. *Con permiso. ¿Cuánto cuesta? ¿Qué es esto? ¿Qué es eso?* Excuse me. How much is it? What is this? What is that?

Lo siento. I'm sorry.

I was a superterranean homesick alien living out of a suitcase. I departed San Francisco on a Saturday with two giant, second-hand rollies and a carry-on bound for Busan. Yet, here we were over two weeks later, their mouths agape, their contents dribbling all over my bedroom floor. I did tape up a vintage National Geographic map of Coastal California by the door and stashed a manila envelope of important documents and favorite photographs in the closet. I put my framed postcard-sized watercolor of Humboldt County's Fern Canyon next to my Raymond Carver, Joan Didion, Haruki Murakami, Lonely Planet South Korea, and Bible on the window sill and squirreled away a bottle of St. George Absinthe to crack in case of emergency. Everything else I just grabbed as needed. Since I was already regretting this move and I could catch a flight out of Gimhae International before anyone would ever notice, why bother to unpack?

* * *

One night I took the village bus across the river into Busan and caught the subway downtown. Up the escalator, I was blinded by the light and disoriented from the constant upward craning of my neck, trying to see the narrow, vertical signs in Hangeul and English attached to the corners of multi-purpose buildings. The signs read:

B1 - a basement *noraebang* (singing room), a Korean "Hof," vintage shop, or "Western" bar.

1F - a coffee house, a chicken restaurant, a *samgyeopsal* (pork belly) restaurant, a convenience store, or a depot of "Pick Me" claw machines stuffed with plush Pikachus, Pink Panthers, and Smurfs.

2F - an international chain restaurant such as Outback, TGI Fridays, Bennigan's, or VIPS.

From the third to ninth floors, a random shuffle of jacks of all trades in no particular order: a dessert cafe, whisky bar, yoga studio, pan-Asian buffet, CrossFit box, blepharoplasty clinic, rhinoplasty clinic, English academy, dental clinic, dance club, "Business Salon." A Business Salon is a place a fresh *waygukin* (foreigner) transplant has no business in. A newbie mistake I learned the hard way.

But I also learned that I arrived in the midst of a renaissance. A vital port city of four million of working-class grit and salt was transforming into a posh metropolis with glass apartment towers eighty floors above the marina below. A welcoming Seoul by the sea on the southeast coast. Natives and expats were eager to introduce me to their favorite places to eat like a local, initiate me at Bohemian coffee shops where poets, comics, and storytellers drew lots for the open-mic, and lead me to dank subterranean taverns where musicians from around the globe came together with native Busanites until six in the morning. Innocuously striking sparks quickly blazing into soju-fueled conflagrations visible from Tsushima.

Farther afield, out of Myeongji and beyond the Bu, I found solace in the mountains, on the islands, or at a simple pension in the countryside replete with soul-refreshing swimming holes and fellow teachers to spend the holidays with. That's why for many years I always knew the expiration of my job contract, apartment contract, and my work visa, but the real ends were hard to find. In fact, I never thought those halcyon days on the peninsula would ever end.

* * *

2019 marked my tenth anniversary of living in Korea. Over the years I've shortened my spells in California between teaching contracts. After my first year, it took me eight months before deciding to return to the ROK. The following year it was five months. Then just a month. Last year, Susanna and I only spent two weeks in the States back in her hometown near Rochester, New York. Yes, you can go home again, but every trip across the Pacific seemed so much farther away than it used to be. And though the setting is mostly the same, people change. Different family and job commitments arise, new interests and priorities. Trips back home now are like Christmas: less magical, more stressful. They no longer feel like a homecoming vacation, but requisite boxes to check to satisfy familial duties and other obligations. While these developments can make one wistful, there's something very disheartening these days, even dangerous: the state of our [dis]union as a nation. Hence, I couldn't see myself moving back to the US anytime soon. Like the old-timey-looking sign I once saw in a North Texas dive bar next to a Greyhound station — "Free beer tomorrow." I'll move back to America next year.

Of course, my wife and I have had plenty of conversations about moving back to the States, often not in accord. She would remind me that she had already started moving her stuff back home before she met me. I would remind her that we both found our first forays in repatriation untenable. I'd say, "you know, Koreans like to brag about their perfect four-season climate, but to me it's always summer. 'Summertime, and the livin' is easy.' We don't have to worry about jobs, housing, health insurance, car insurance, or commutes. And didn't we expats choose this — to be distant from the burdens and vexations of living in America?"

* * *

But that all changed recently when I went to the doctor with Susanna. We walked over to the Jamo Women's Hospital near our place. It was her third visit for her pregnancy but the first time I could accompany her. We walked up the stairs to the second floor into a narrow hallway and a lobby packed with Korean women sporting various sized paunches. There were just as many female nurses as patients, and the staff dressed in pastel pink and teal scrubs. One middle-aged Korean lady really stood out with her belly protruding under a purple cotton muumuu of a knee-length t-shirt that said in big green letters, "I'M SHY . . ." on the front, "BUT I'VE GOT A BIG DICK/Carlos' n Charlie's/Cancun, Mexico" on the back. My wife was trying not to laugh too hard while I was just trying to stay out of the way. Susanna was directed to take a seat over on a row of benches outside an enclave of plain brown wooden office doors and was told to "wait for the Number Five doctor."

We waited about five minutes before a nurse invited us into Number Five doctor's room. He was an older gentleman who had a way of smiling while speaking softly at the same time. He made small talk with me while my wife was in a little adjacent room with the nurse next to the doctor's desk behind a thin curtain. He assured me to just relax and have a seat.

Then I saw that a flat screen on the wall next to his desk facing me had been turned on. Just like my wife, the doctor, and the nurse, I could see the ultrasound images, too, which I thought were like a movie. I told Susanna from the beginning, I don't want to know. I want to be surprised. Since she was only seventeen weeks at the time, I didn't think I'd be able to see much or know which sex the baby would be anyway. Or I thought at least the doctor would ask us if we wanted to know. But I guess that's not how it works in Korea. Or maybe this was just one of those common occurrences that happens when very limited language skills lead to such miscommunication.

The Number Five doctor went right to work. I could hear him from behind the curtain. I guess he was pointing things on the screen out for Sus. "Ok. Head good. Body. Heart. Arm. Leg. Female baby."

I heard the doctor loud and clear but my wife prompted him to say it again. "Head. Body. Heart. Arm. Leg. Female baby," in exactly the same tone.

"You hear that, Ant?" she asked from the other room.

Stunned, I nodded my head a couple of times before softly responding, "Yeah."

*　*　*

Students here have a real knack for going straight to the personal when given an opportunity to ask questions of their foreign teacher. Where are you from? How old are you? Are you married? If yes, is your wife Korean? Do you have a baby? Do you want a baby? Do you want a boy or girl? Often these questions are asked before even asking, "What's your name?"

I remember earlier in the year, before she was pregnant, one of my wife's fifth-grade students said, "You should have a baby in America so the baby looks American. You have a baby in Korea, it will look Korean."

After I broke the news to my best friend Big T that we were expecting, after the congratulations and how the doctor spilled the beans, I told him about what Susanna's student advised on where to have a baby. That fifth-grader still cracks me up. But Big T said, "Why are you laughing? I feel the same way about this shit! Why are you having the baby there?"

* * *

Well, at this point, let me just get right to it and explain why. Not just why we're having a baby here but, also, why I'm beginning to see the end here after nearly ten years of living in Korea. It's not just about health care in the USA versus ROK, but facts are cold and they're simply facts. As NPR reported under the headline "How Hospitals Can Tackle The Maternal Mortality Crisis," Mara Gordon writes:

"Having a baby in the United States can be dangerous. American women are more likely than women in any other developed country to die during childbirth or from pregnancy-related complications.

And while other countries' maternal death rates have gone down, U.S. rates have risen since 2000, a fact that has left both doctors and expectant mothers concerned about the state of maternity care in this country."

So there's that. There's also the benefit of two months paid maternity leave, or even more if my wife wants it from her school, and the national government-issued debit card worth ₩500,000 to help cover our costs. Though that does not mean that our daughter will have dual citizenship automatically bestowed upon birth, that's still nearly five hundred reasons to stay. But that consideration of citizenship presages exactly why we are planning on moving back to our native ground.

* * *

I remember waiting for a flight at SFO with my parents in September of 2009. I bought a *Lonely Planet South Korea* guide, the current *Atlantic Monthly*, and *The Economist* from the Hudson News shop at the terminal. On the flight I read an article from one of those magazines (don't remember which exactly), about what makes America so admired, so respected, how the proverbial beacon of hope and light is its diversity. The author described what makes the United States very special: anyone can be American. He had spent nearly twenty years in Japan, and though one could be fluent in the language, unless one is born in Japan of Japanese heritage, no one can ever be Japanese. This is also true in Korea. Susanna, me, our child, will always be, even if we all live our entire (God willing) long lives here, we will always be *waygukin* to Koreans. Foreigners.

While I understand that the States has a serious dysfunction due to increasing tribalism undermining the bedrock of America's foundation once built on the strength of immigrants, and I'm writing this now at a time when brown families are being separated, incarcerated in different camps in conditions much worse than Manzanar, as this father considers how the opponents of his daughter's future run for Congress or President will incite those so-called patriots' vile chants of "Send her back! Send her back!" or "Lock her up! Lock her up!"; despite the US's pitiful record regarding race relations and its inability to stem the spread of hate and gun violence, coming from a decade spent living in a homogenous country like Korea, I've realized and can truly appreciate how colorful America is. I still believe in her ideals, her strength through unity *and* diversity. How beautiful she really can be. We're not giving up on this.

Also, there's something even more tangible that I hope our baby girl will understand someday. Her blood carries traces of the field dust that clings to brown sweaty brows in a long San Joaquin Valley Indian summer. Her bones ossify with fossilized seashells and ammonites unearthed by the Pleistocene glacial activity that carved Watkins Glen and Western New York's river gorges. Her family tree is deeply rooted in a composite of Tulare Lake silt and loam, Finger Lakes slate and shale. These elements transcend any citizenry, nationality, or birthplace, and are essential to her family's origin story. That's why we're coming home.

Like the ultrasound images of this life growing inside my wife's womb, with each visit to her obstetrician, my life is becoming clearer, more defined. While there's still a great distance between me and my destination (a return to the States, a home for my family, maybe out in the country, definitely with some dogs), it's now easier to see the ends. Or, at the very least, the beginning of things. Everything really.

Acknowledgments

The author is grateful to the editors of the following literary journals who first published these essays: "World Cup Identity" (*Foreign Literary Journal*), "As-Salaam Alaikum, Moustafa" (*Stone Canoe*), "Frequently Asked Questions about Staying Safe in South Korea" (*Mount Hope*), "Annyeong to All That" (*Touchstone Literary Magazine*).

Creator's Bio

Anthony Huerta Velasquez hails from the San Joaquin Valley of California. His creative nonfiction essays appeared in *Hunger Mountain*, *Mount Hope*, *Concho River Review*, *Sierra Nevada Review*, *South Dakota Review*, *Roanoke Review*, *Stone Canoe*, *Touchstone*, *Panorama*, *Past Ten*, and *The Offbeat*. After spending a decade in Busan, South Korea, he now calls the Finger Lakes region of New York home.

www.ingramcontent.com/pod-product-compliance
Lightning Source LLC
Chambersburg PA
CBHW030527130626
46549CB00007B/3123